Piano • Vocal • Guitar

A Very Merry Christmas

ISBN 0-634-00938-9

HAL•LEONARD®
CORPORATION

7777 W. BLUEMOUND RD. P.O. BOX 13819 MILWAUKEE, WI 53213

Visit Hal Leonard Online at
www.halleonard.com

ALL I WANT FOR CHRISTMAS IS YOU

Words and Music by MARIAH CAREY
and WALTER AFANASIEFF

4

As Long As There's Christmas

from Walt Disney's BEAUTY AND THE BEAST - THE ENCHANTED CHRISTMAS

Music by RACHEL PORTMAN
Lyrics by DON BLACK

BLUE CHRISTMAS

Words and Music by BILLY HAYES
and JAY JOHNSON

CAROL FOR A CHRISTMAS TREE

Music by LEE HOLDRIDGE

Lyrically; not too fast and delicately

CHRISTMAS IS ALL IN THE HEART

Words and Music by
STEVEN CURTIS CHAPMAN

THE CHRISTMAS SONG
(Chestnuts Roasting on an Open Fire)

Music and Lyric by MEL TORME
and ROBERT WELLS

DO THEY KNOW IT'S CHRISTMAS?

Medium Rock

Words and Music by M. URE
and B. GELDOF

It's Christ - mas - time, there's no need to be a - fraid.__

At Christ - mas - time, we let in light__ and we ban - ish shade.__

And in our world__ of plen - ty_____ we can spread a smile__ of joy.__

COLD DECEMBER NIGHTS

Words and Music by MICHAEL McCARY
and SHAWN STOCKMAN

Why aren't __ you next __ to me _____ cel - e - brat - ing

DO YOU HEAR WHAT I HEAR

Words and Music by NOEL REGNEY
and GLORIA SHAYNE

Moderately, with feeling

FELIZ NAVIDAD

Music and Lyrics by
JOSE FELICIANO

THE GIFT

Words and Music by TOM DOUGLAS
and JIM BRICKMAN

Slow ballad

Female: Hoo.

Win-ter snow is fall-ing down, chil-dren laugh-ing all a-round,

lights are turn-ing on, like a fair-y tale come true.

THE GREATEST GIFT OF ALL

Words and Music by
JOHN JARVIS

GOING HOME FOR CHRISTMAS

Words and Music by STEVEN CURTIS CHAPMAN
and JAMES ISAAC ELLIOT

GRANDMA GOT RUN OVER BY A REINDEER

Words and Music by
RANDY BROOKS

Moderately bright

Grand-ma got run o-ver by a rein-deer walk-ing home from our house Christ-mas Eve.

You can say there's no such thing as San-ta, but as for me and Grand-pa, we be-

You can say there's no such thing as San-ta, but as for me and Grand-pa, we be -

lieve.

Additional Lyrics

Verse 2:
Now we're all so proud of Grandpa,
He's been taking this so well.
See him in there watching football,
Drinking beer and playing cards with Cousin Mel.
It's not Christmas without Grandma.
All the family's dressed in black,
And we just can't help but wonder:
Should we open up her gifts or send them back?
Chorus

Verse 3:
Now the goose is on the table,
And the pudding made of fig,
And the blue and silver candles,
That would just have matched the hair in Grandma's wig.
I've warned all my friends and neighbors,
Better watch out for yourselves.
They should never give a license
To a man who drives a sleigh and plays with elves.
Chorus

GROWN-UP CHRISTMAS LIST

Words and Music by DAVID FOSTER
and LINDA THOMPSON-JENNER

I'LL BE HOME FOR CHRISTMAS

Words and Music by KIM GANNON
and WALTER KENT

I'm dream-ing to-night of a place I love, __ e-ven more than I u-sual-ly do. And al-though I know it's a long road back, __ I prom-ise you

HAPPY XMAS
(War Is Over)

Words and Music by JOHN LENNON
and YOKO ONO

84

I SAW MOMMY KISSING SANTA CLAUS

Words and Music by
TOMMIE CONNOR

I saw Mom-my kiss-ing San-ta Claus, un-der-neath the mis-tle-toe last night. She did-n't see me creep down the stairs to have a peep, she thought that I was tucked up in my bed-room fast a-

JINGLE-BELL ROCK

Words and Music by JOE BEAL
and JIM BOOTHE

LAST CHRISTMAS

Words and Music by
GEORGE MICHAEL

Fmaj7/G   G7   [1] Fmaj7/G   G7   [2] Fmaj7/G   G7

D.S. al Coda
(with repeat)

kissed me now___ I know you'd fool me a - gain.___
found a real___ love. You'll nev - er   fool me a - gain.___

CODA   Fmaj7/G   G7   Cmaj9   C6

- cial.   A face   on a lov - er with a

Cmaj9   C6   Em7/A   Am7

fire in his heart,___   a man un - der cov - er but you

Em7/A   Am7   Am7/D   Dm7   Am7/D   Dm7

tore him a - part.___   May - be   next year   I'll

LET IT SNOW

Words and Music by WANYA MORRIS
and BRIAN McKNIGHT

MIRACLES

By KENNY G
and WALTER AFANASIEFF

Slowly, tenderly

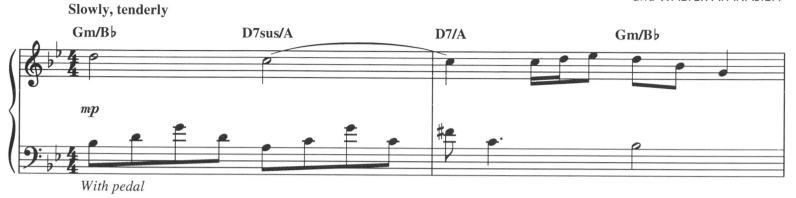

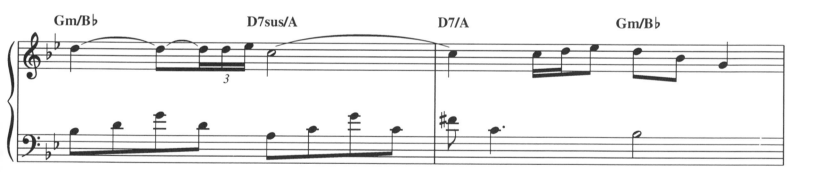

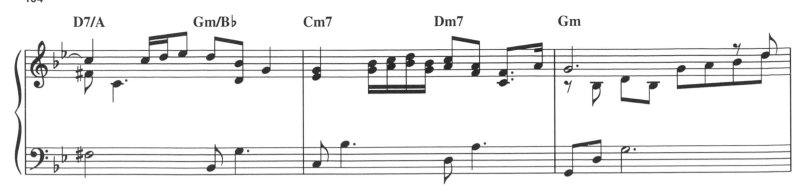

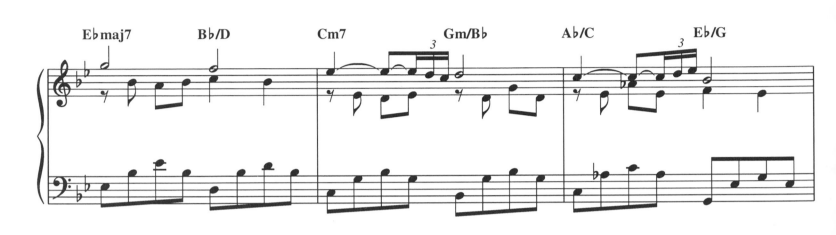

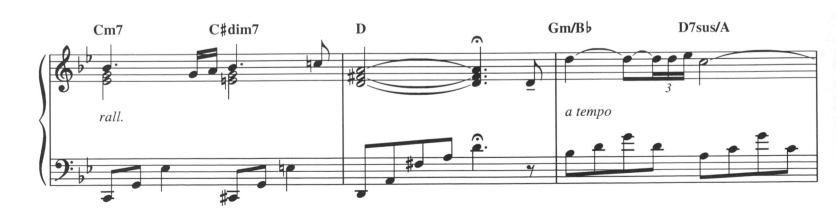

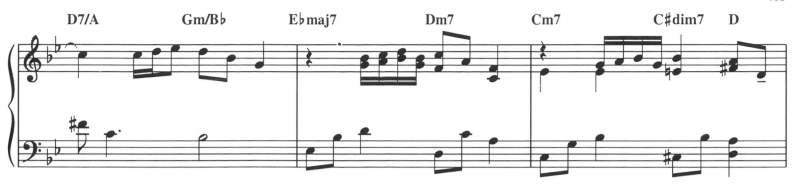

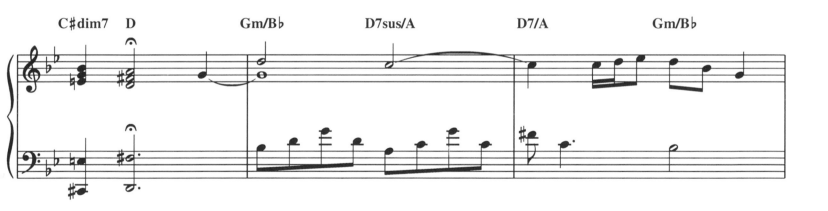

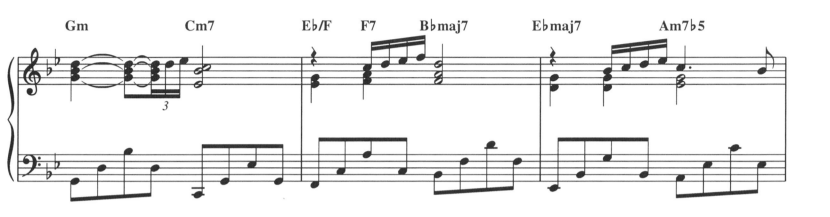

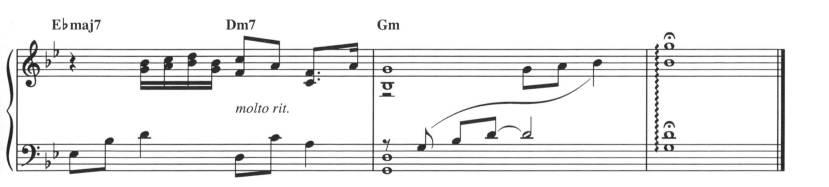

MERRY CHRISTMAS, BABY

Words and Music by LOU BAXTER
and JOHNNY MOORE

MISS YOU MOST AT CHRISTMAS TIME

Words and Music by MARIAH CAREY
and WALTER AFANASIEFF

THE MOST WONDERFUL TIME OF THE YEAR

Words and Music by EDDIE POLA
and GEORGE WYLE

NOËL: CHRISTMAS EVE, 1913

Music by LEE HOLDRIDGE
Lyric by ROBERT BRIDGES*

*Guitarists: Chords are played finger style.

121

O JOYFUL CHILDREN

Music by LEE HOLDRIDGE
Words by MARY HUCKABY

PLEASE COME HOME FOR CHRISTMAS

Words and Music by CHARLES BROWN
and GENE REDD

PRETTY PAPER

Words and Music by
WILLIE NELSON

ROCKIN' AROUND THE CHRISTMAS TREE

Music and Lyrics by
JOHNNY MARKS

RUDOLPH THE RED-NOSED REINDEER

Music and Lyrics by
JOHNNY MARKS

SANTA CLAUS IS BACK IN TOWN

Words and Music by JERRY LEIBER
and MIKE STOLLER

SANTA, BRING MY BABY BACK
(To Me)

Words and Music by CLAUDE DeMETRUIS
and AARON SCHROEDER

CHORUS

Don't need a lot of pres-ents to make my Christ-mas
Christ-mas tree is read-y, the can-dles all a-

bright. But I just need my ba-by's arms
glow, with my ba-by far a-way what

wound a-round me tight. Oh, San-ta, hear my plea. _____
good is mis-tle-toe?

SHAKE ME I RATTLE
(Squeeze Me I Cry)

Words and Music by HAL HACKADY
and CHARLES NAYLOR

Moderately Slow

Lyrics:

I was pass-ing by a toy shop on the
called an-oth-er toy shop on a
late and snow was fall-ing as the

cor-ner of the Square, where a lit-tle girl was
square so long a-go Where I saw a lit-tle
shop-pers hur-ried by Past the girl ie at the

look-ing in the win-dow there She was
dol-ly that I want-ed so I re-
win-dow with her lit-tle head held high They were

SHARE LOVE

Words and Music by
NATHAN MORRIS

SILVER BELLS

from the Paramount Picture THE LEMON DROP KID

Words and Music by JAY LIVINGSTON
and RAY EVANS

THERE'S A NEW KID IN TOWN

Words and Music by CURLY PUTMAN,
DON COOK and KEITH WHITLEY

look-ing for the king, _____ the new Mes -
see you've trav-eled far _____ bear-ing

si - ah. _____ We're
treas - ures. _____ You

WONDERFUL CHRISTMASTIME

Words and Music by
McCARTNEY